Only love can break a heart, but a shoe sale can come close

Other Cathy® Books from Andrews and McMeel

Only love can break a heart, but a shoe sale can come close

A  Collection

by Cathy Guisewite

Andrews and McMeel
A Universal Press Syndicate Company
Kansas City

OUR GRANDPARENTS' GENERATION KEPT THEIR STRESS IN THEIR HEADS, GOT HEADACHES, AND CARRIED ON WITH LIFE.

OUR PARENTS' GENERATION SENT THEIR STRESS TO THEIR STOMACHS, GOT ULCERS, AND WALKED AROUND WITH STOMACHACHES.

OUR GENERATION JAMS OUR STRESS INTO OUR BACKS, CREATING A CYCLE OF EXPANDING, EXCRUCIATING PAIN THAT AFFECTS EVERY MUSCLE GROUP AND DEBILITATES THE ENTIRE BODY.

THE LEGACY OF THE BABY-BOOMERS, SUMMED UP IN JUST FIVE LITTLE WORDS....

TOP THIS, CLASS OF 1990!

I'M SORRY YOU HURT YOUR BACK, IRVING, AND WANT TO OFFER MY SUPPORT.

I WILL HELP YOU APPROACH THIS WITH PATIENCE, DIGNITY, STRENGTH AND....

FOOD! YOU NEED FOOD! IT'S A CRISIS! GET SOME FOOD! FOOD! FOOD! FOOD!

INCREDIBLE.

I KNOW. I WAS HERE A FULL FIVE MINUTES BEFORE MY MOTHER'S VOICE KICKED IN.

"MANY PEOPLE TENSE THEIR BACK MUSCLES INSTEAD OF EXPRESSING ANXIETIES AND FEARS, WHICH WEAKENS THE MUSCLES AND MAKES THE BACK VULNERABLE TO INJURIES."... THIS IS YOU, IRVING!

THAT ISN'T ME, CATHY.

"BACK PAIN IS CAUSED NOT SO MUCH FROM LIFTING ONE THING WRONG AS IT IS FROM A LIFETIME OF DENYING FEELINGS BY CLENCHING THE BACK."....THIS IS YOU!

THAT IS NOT ME!

NOT ME! NOT ME! NOT ME!

BAM BAM BAM

...OUCH.

"EMOTIONAL PAIN THAT GOES UN-ACKNOWLEDGED WILL SURFACE SOMEWHERE AS PHYSICAL PAIN..."

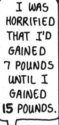

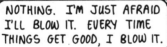

7

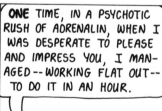

I HAVE GRABBED THE ONE PAIR OF PANTYHOSE THAT DOESN'T HAVE A RUN OUT OF A DRAWER STUFFED WITH 36 RUINED PAIRS!

I HAVE REACHED INTO THE REFRIGERATOR AND PULLED OUT THE ONE THING THAT PROBABLY WON'T POISON ME!

I HAVE STUCK MY HAND IN A 50-POUND PURSE AND LOCATED TWO DROPS OF CONTACT SOLUTION, AN EARRING BACK, AND A TUBE OF LIPSTICK THAT DOESN'T HAVE A BREATH MINT JAMMED IN IT!

...AND NOW I'M CELEBRATING THE FACT THAT, OUT OF ALL OF LIFE'S LITTLE VICTORIES, THERE ARE SOME WE GET TO ENJOY WITHOUT AN AUDIENCE....

AUGUST 1990: COUPLES ARE FLINGING THEMSELVES INTO INVOLVEMENT... IRVING AND I ARE STILL TIPTOEING AROUND THE EDGE.

COUPLES ARE MASHED TOGETHER TRYING ANYTHING TO MAKE A RELATIONSHIP WORK... IRVING AND I ARE STILL FLUTTERING BACK AND FORTH, NEVER QUITE GETTING THAT CLOSE.

IN A WORLD FULL OF LAMBADA, WE'RE STILL DOING BALLET.

WHEN MY HUSBAND SEES THE BILL FOR THIS, HE'S GOING TO KILL ME! HA, HA!

WHEN MY BOYFRIEND SEES THE BILL FOR THIS, HE'S GOING TO KILL ME! HA, HA!

WHEN I SEE THE BILL FOR THIS, I'M GOING TO KILL MYSELF! HA, HA!!

...WHY DO I ALWAYS HAVE TO DO EVERYTHING ALONE??

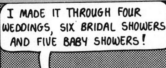

MARLA: SPENT TWO-WEEK VACATION AND ENTIRE VISA CREDIT LIMIT ON 2,000-MILE SIGHTSEEING TOUR WITH HUSBAND, MOTHER-IN-LAW, THREE SCREAMING CHILDREN AND 4,500 FOOD WRAPPERS SQUASHED IN CAR.

DANIEL: CASHED IN I.R.A. AND ALL BONUS MILES TO FLY NOW-EX-GIRLFRIEND TO EXOTIC ISLAND FOR ROMANTIC TRYST THAT WAS TECHNICALLY OVER 14 MINUTES INTO THE TRIP.

CATHY: USED ALL VACATION TIME ORGANIZING CLOSETS LAST WINTER. NEXT CONCEIVABLE TIME OFF IS CALLING IN SICK THE DAY AFTER HALLOWEEN.

MR. PINKLEY: MADE THE MISTAKE OF ASKING IF EVERYONE WAS WELL-RESTED AND READY TO GET BACK TO WORK.

17

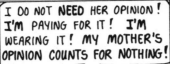

WHY DON'T YOU LET YOUR MOTHER TAKE A PEEK?

I DO NOT WANT MY MOTHER'S OPINION.

I DO NOT **NEED** HER OPINION! I'M PAYING FOR IT! I'M WEARING IT! MY MOTHER'S OPINION COUNTS FOR NOTHING!

SHE WOULDN'T LIKE IT.

I HAVEN'T BEEN ALLOWED TO THE POLLS IN TEN YEARS, BUT I STILL CAST THE WINNING VOTE.

THAT WON'T REALLY LOOK RIGHT WITHOUT MATCHING TIGHTS.

COULD YOU BRING SOME IN?

OH, MY, NO! TIGHTS ARE DOWNSTAIRS IN HOSIERY. YOU CAN BUY THE OUTFIT AND TAKE IT DOWN TO THE TIGHTS....

OR BUY THE TIGHTS DOWNSTAIRS, THE SHOES ON LEVEL 3, THE BELT ON LEVEL 5, THE CAMISOLE ON 6, AND THE JEWELRY ON 2 AND THEN HAUL IT ALL IN HERE AND SEE IF ANY OF IT HAPPENS TO MATCH!

...ANOTHER HAPPY CUSTOMER, ENJOYING THE CONVENIENCE OF SHOPPING IN A DEPARTMENT STORE.

DO YOU HAVE THIS IN BLACK?

BLACK IS OUT. TOO HIGH-TECH. TOTALLY IMPERSONAL.

NEW

FAIL

THIS YEAR WE'RE WEARING THE WARM, ENVIRONMENTALLY AWARE COLORS OF THE RAINFORESTS, THE SOIL, AND THE BABBLING BROOKS!

EACH NEW EARTH-TONED OUTFIT SENDS A MESSAGE THAT WE CARE ABOUT THE DWINDLING RESOURCES OF THE PLANET!

WOULDN'T WE SEND A STRONGER MESSAGE BY JUST RE-WEARING THE CLOTHES WE ALREADY OWN?

CAN WE GET THIS IN BLACK?

I NEED MY PARKING TICKET VALIDATED, PLEASE.

DID YOU MAKE A PURCHASE?

I'VE JUST SPENT TWO HOURS SEARCHING FOR ONE TOP TO MATCH A SKIRT I BOUGHT LAST YEAR THAT WAS SUPPOSED TO "GO WITH EVERYTHING"... THEN WAITED IN LINE FOR 20 MINUTES FOR A PUNY DRESSING ROOM WITH A DISTORTED MIRROR ONLY TO FIND THE ONE THING THAT LOOKED HALFWAY DECENT HAD A GIANT RIP THAT THE SALESCLERK TRIED TO CONVINCE ME WAS "PART OF THE CHARM."

NO, I DID NOT MAKE A PURCHASE!

ONE MOMENT, PLEASE.

DO WE VALIDATE FOR AGGRAVATION?

OUR LIPS ARE WRONG.

OUR LIPS ARE WRONG?

OUR LIPS ARE SHINY. THEY'RE SUPPOSED TO BE MATTE.

I THOUGHT THE EYELIDS WERE MATTE.

NO. EYELIDS ARE SHIMMERY. LASHES ARE GLISTENY. LINER IS MISTY. CHEEKS ARE DEWY.

THE LIPS HAVE TO BE MATTE.

IT SEEMS LIKE A LOT TO REMEMBER FOR SOMETHING THAT ONLY STAYS ON MY FACE FOR TEN MINUTES.

AREN'T YOU SEEING IRVING TONIGHT, CATHY?

NO. WE DON'T WANT TO GET BACK INTO THE "SEEING EACH OTHER EVERY NIGHT" RUT.

OF COURSE, WE ALSO DON'T WANT TO GET INTO THE "ME WAITING FOR HIM TO CALL" RUT... THE "HIM WAITING FOR ME TO CALL" RUT... THE "NOT CALLING AT ALL" RUT... OR THE "CALLING TEN TIMES A DAY" RUT.

WE'RE IN THE "IN BETWEEN RUTS" RUT.

AS ENVIRONMENTAL AWARENESS RISES, WE PAUSE TO ASK WHAT IT IS THAT MOVES PEOPLE FROM SIMPLY AGREEING THAT SOMETHING HAS TO BE DONE TO DOING SOMETHING THEMSELVES.

WHAT DOES IT TAKE? ONE MORE RAINFOREST RALLY? ONE MORE EARTH DAY SPECIAL? ONE MORE OZONE BROCHURE?

OR IS IT SOMETIMES THE WORKINGS OF SOME MORE INTANGIBLE, PERSONAL FORCE....

I'M RECYCLING!

WHO IS SHE, AND WHAT HAVE YOU BEEN SHARING WITH HER BESIDES YOUR GARBAGE??!!

IRVING, IF YOU'RE NOT SEEING SOMEONE ELSE, WHO DREW LITTLE HEARTS ALL OVER YOUR RECYCLING CANS?

OH, THAT WAS JULIA!

JULIA? YOUR EX-GIRLFRIEND, JULIA??

YEAH. HA, HA! SHE JUST CALLED ME OUT OF THE BLUE!

A WOMAN YOU DUMPED FOUR YEARS AGO CALLED, CAME OVER, AND DREW HEARTS ON YOUR TRASH CANS AND YOU THINK IT WAS "OUT OF THE BLUE"?!

WE ALWAYS SAID WE'D BE FRIENDS!

WHY CAN I SEE SO CLEARLY WHAT OTHER WOMEN ARE UP TO, AND YET NEVER HAVE A CLUE ABOUT WHAT I'M DOING?

JULIA JUST WANTED TO HELP ME SET UP A RECYCLING SYSTEM, CATHY.

SHE'S AFTER YOU, IRVING.

SHE IS NOT AFTER ME!

OH, YES SHE IS! SHE WANTS YOU! SHE MISSES YOU! SHE'S LUSTING AFTER YOU!

IRVING, A WOMAN DOES NOT CALL AFTER FOUR YEARS UNLESS SHE'S DESPERATE TO BE IN YOUR ARMS AGAIN!

...REALLY? DESPERATE?? REALLY??

...AND APPARENTLY I'M GOING TO HELP HER GET THERE.

21

IN PARIS:
PATTERNED TIGHTS,
OVERSIZED TOP.

IN MILAN:
PATTERNED TIGHTS,
OVERSIZED TOP.

IN LONDON:
PATTERNED TIGHTS,
OVERSIZED TOP.

IN MY BATHROOM:
PATTERNED TIGHTS,
OVERSIZED TOP.

24

IF I DON'T MAKE A BIG DEAL ABOUT IRVING SEEING JULIA, IT WILL DEMEAN HOW MUCH HE MEANS TO ME, PUT MORE DISTANCE BETWEEN US, AND TRASH OUR FUTURE TOGETHER.

IF I **DO** MAKE A BIG DEAL ABOUT JULIA, I MIGHT MAKE MORE OF IT THAN IT REALLY IS, START A FIGHT FOR NOTHING, AND TRASH OUR FUTURE TOGETHER.

IF I **SORT OF** MAKE A BIG DEAL AND SORT OF **DON'T** MAKE A BIG DEAL, I'LL COME OFF AS AN IRRATIONAL NAG, AGGRAVATE US BOTH, AND TRASH OUR FUTURE TOGETHER.

AT LEAST FOR ONCE IN MY LIFE I DON'T HAVE TO ASK WHERE OUR RELATIONSHIP IS GOING.

WE NEED TO TALK ABOUT YOUR EX-GIRLFRIEND JULIA, IRVING.

NOT THIS AGAIN...

IF WE'RE NOT TALKING ABOUT JULIA, I'M AFRAID YOU'RE SITTING THERE **THINKING** ABOUT JULIA WITHOUT ME KNOWING IT.

AT LEAST IF WE'RE TALKING ABOUT HER SHE'S OUT HERE IN THE ROOM WITH US INSTEAD OF INSIDE YOUR BRAIN WHERE I DON'T KNOW WHAT'S GOING ON !!

FINE. JULIA! JULIA! JULIA! THERE! ARE YOU SATISFIED?!

WHO ELSE IS IN THERE THAT I DON'T KNOW ABOUT?

IS A "POST-IT" NOTE RECYCLABLE OR NOT BECAUSE IT HAS GLUE ON IT?

I DON'T KNOW. WHAT ABOUT PAPERS WITH A STAPLE IN THEM?

I DON'T KNOW. WHAT ABOUT AN ENVELOPE WITH A STAMP ON IT?

I DON'T KNOW. HOW ABOUT A PUFFY MAILER WITH A SHINY LABEL?

TO THE RESOURCE LIBRARY!

TO THE BOOKSTORE!

TO THE ECO-HOTLINE!

HEY! IT'S 10:00 IN THE MORNING! GET BACK HERE!

MY STAFF: MAKING THE WORLD A BETTER PLACE IN WHICH TO BE UNEMPLOYED.

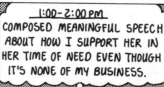

6:00–11:00AM
WORRIED ABOUT CATHY.

11:00–1:00PM
LISTENED TO LECTURE FROM CATHY'S FATHER ABOUT HOW WHATEVER'S BOTHERING CATHY IS NONE OF MY BUSINESS.

1:00–2:00PM
COMPOSED MEANINGFUL SPEECH ABOUT HOW I SUPPORT HER IN HER TIME OF NEED EVEN THOUGH IT'S NONE OF MY BUSINESS.

2:00–3:00PM
BOUGHT GROCERIES IN CASE CATHY WANTS TO COME OVER AND DISCUSS SOMETHING.

3:00–5:30PM
REHEARSED SPEECH.

5:30–8:45PM
TAPED SHOWS THAT COULD APPLY TO A VARIETY OF SITUATIONS THAT COULD BE BOTHERING CATHY.

8:45–11:00PM
WORRIED ABOUT CATHY.

ONCE AGAIN, I'M TOTALLY PREPARED FOR THE FINAL EXAM AND I HAVE NO IDEA WHAT THE SUBJECT IS YET.

YOUR MOTHER FEELS TERRIBLE WHEN YOU LEAVE HER OUT OF YOUR LIFE.

OH, MOM, I'M SORRY, BUT...

YOUR FATHER WISHES YOU'D GO TO HIM LIKE YOU USED TO WHEN YOU WERE LITTLE.

OH, DAD, I'M SORRY, BUT...

I'M SORRY, MOM...

I'M SORRY, DAD...

I'M SORRY, MOM...

I'M SORRY, DAD...

OKAY! ENOUGH! ENOUGH! I'LL TALK!!

DIZZINESS THERAPY STRIKES AGAIN!

SMACK!

WE NEED TO DISCUSS THE "M" WORD BECAUSE I'M GETTING A LITTLE ANXIOUS ABOUT THE "B" WORD, IRVING.

IF YOU CAN'T DEAL WITH THE "M" WORD, I'LL HAVE NO CHOICE BUT TO BRING UP THE "R" WORD, THE "T" WORD AND THE "E" WORD, WHICH WILL ONLY LEAD TO THE "Q" WORD...
...AND I DON'T THINK I HAVE TO MENTION WHAT WILL HAPPEN IF THE CONVERSATION DETERIORATES INTO THE "J" WORD!

THINK ABOUT IT, HONEY.

DO THEY STAY UP AT NIGHT INVENTING NEW WAYS TO TORTURE US, OR WHAT?

28

29

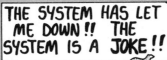

I GAVE HER ONE KNOWING GLANCE INSTEAD OF WEIGHING HER DOWN WITH THE FULL "LOOK"...

I GAVE HER A FEW POIGNANT REMARKS INSTEAD OF A WHOLE SPEECH...

I GAVE HER A REASSURING HUG INSTEAD OF A SUFFOCATING EMBRACE...

"MOTHERING-LITE": ALL THE ESSENTIAL INGREDIENTS, NONE OF THE SATISFACTION.

YOUR FATHER AND I HAVE WORRIED ABOUT YOUR FINANCES, BUT OF COURSE WE DIDN'T WANT TO SAY ANYTHING.

EVEN WHEN WE **WANTED** TO SAY SOMETHING, WE FELT WE SHOULDN'T SAY ANYTHING.

NOW THAT WE MAYBE **SHOULD** SAY SOMETHING, THERE'S REALLY NOTHING WE CAN SAY EXCEPT WHAT WE COULD HAVE SAID BEFORE WHICH WE COULDN'T SAY THEN AND SEEMS POINTLESS TO SAY NOW.

DOES THIS FAMILY KNOW HOW TO COMMUNICATE, OR WHAT?

SHE DRIVES HER PARTIALLY PAID-FOR CAR TO HER PARTIALLY PAID-FOR HOME...

THROWS ON HER PARTIALLY PAID-FOR SWEATSUIT...CLICKS ON HER PARTIALLY PAID-FOR LAMP...PUTS HER FEET ON HER PARTIALLY PAID-FOR COFFEE TABLE...

...WATCHES HER PARTIALLY PAID-FOR TV WHILE SHE HAS DINNER AND FORMS ONE PARTIALLY COHERENT THOUGHT...

I'VE JUST EATEN THE ONLY THING IN MY LIFE I ACTUALLY OWNED.

35

38

BETH: SPENT HOLIDAY WEEKEND BUYING ALL CHRISTMAS GIFTS AND LOVINGLY PACKING THEM FOR MAIL IN HOMEMADE RECYCLABLE WRAP.

KAREN: SPENT HOLIDAY WEEKEND PLACING CATALOG GIFT ORDERS AND ORGANIZING ENTIRE HOME AND WARDROBE FOR CHRISTMAS SEASON.

MARTHA: SPENT HOLIDAY WEEKEND UPDATING ADDRESSES IN COMPUTER, PRINTING LABELS AND ENCLOSING CUTE PERSONAL NOTES IN CHRISTMAS CARDS.

CATHY: SPENT HOLIDAY WEEKEND WITH HER MOTHER.

41

THIS MAKES A LOVELY GIFT AND IT'S 35% OFF!

35% OFF? HOO, BOY! YOU MUST BE PANICKED ABOUT SLOW SALES THIS CHRISTMAS!

WE ARE **NOT** PANICKED!

NO? I THINK I'LL WAIT 'TILL YOU MARK IT DOWN 45%!...NO! MAKE THAT **60%** OFF!

BETTER YET, IF YOU WANT TO MOVE SOME MERCHANDISE THIS HOLIDAY SEASON, **PAY** ME TO TAKE IT OFF YOUR HANDS!!

DECEMBER 5, AND THE RETAILER'S SENSE OF HUMOR IS ALREADY SLASHED BY 95%.

YOU'LL HAVE TO GO TO THE GIFT WRAP DEPARTMENT FOR YOUR COMPLIMENTARY BOX.

OH, NO! THERE'S ALWAYS A HUGE LINE!

I **HATE** WAITING IN LINE! I'M A VERY BUSY PERSON! WHY SHOULD **I** HAVE TO WAIT IN LINE LIKE EVERYONE ELSE??!

HELLO, GIFT WRAP? I'M SENDING OVER A VERY SPECIAL CUSTOMER! **CLEAR A PATH!**

THANK YOU.

...THEN HIDE ALL THE BOXES, SHUT YOUR LITTLE WINDOW AND GO OUT TO LUNCH BEFORE SHE GETS THERE!

WOMAN ATTEMPTING TO STAY ON A DIET DURING THE HOLIDAYS WITHOUT CRACKING:

WOMAN ATTEMPTING TO STAY ON A **BUDGET** DURING THE HOLIDAYS WITHOUT CRACKING:

WOMAN ATTEMPTING TO STAY ON A DIET **AND** A BUDGET DURING THE HOLIDAYS WITHOUT CRACKING:

WOMAN CRACKING:

JOY TO THE WORLD!!

44

47

IN THE '70s, THE EMERGENCE OF THE MALL SHOPPER:

I CAN WALK TO EVERY STORE IN A NICE, WARM, CHEERFUL ENVIRONMENT!

IN THE '80s, THE EMERGENCE OF THE CATALOG SHOPPER:

I CAN ORDER ALL MY GIFTS FROM THE COMFORT OF MY HOME!

IN THE '90s, THE EMERGENCE OF THE-SHOPPER-WHO-HAULS-HER-CATALOGS-TO-THE-MALL-TRYING-TO-FIND-WHAT-SHE-WISHED-SHE'D-ORDERED-A-MONTH-AGO:

ITEM #1432-F! I MUST HAVE ITEM #1432-F!

THIS IS A "BED AND BATH BOUTIQUE"! THAT IS A MAIL-ORDER FRUIT CATALOG!!

STACKS OF GIFT CATALOGS IN THE OFFICE...STACKS OF GIFT CATALOGS AT HOME... WHY DIDN'T I SHOP WITH GIFT CATALOGS THIS YEAR???

IT WOULD HAVE BEEN SO EASY! IT WOULD HAVE BEEN SO FAST!! WHY DIDN'T I JUST DO IT? WHY? WHY?!

YOU STILL CAN, CATHY! THEY ALL HAVE TOLL-FREE ORDER LINES AND THEY'LL SHIP OVERNIGHT. YOU COULD HAVE EVERYTHING HERE TOMORROW!

NAH... I THINK I'LL LOOK AROUND IN THE STORES A LITTLE MORE FIRST...

IS THE PACKAGING BIO-DEGRADABLE? ARE ANY OZONE-DEPLETING CHEMICALS RELEASED IN THE MANU-FACTURING PROCESS?

IS IT MADE IN A COUNTRY WHICH CONDONES ANY IN-HUMANE PRACTICES? BY BUY-ING THIS, WOULD I IN ANY WAY BE INADVERTENTLY SUP-PORTING ANY COMPANY IN-VOLVED IN ANIMAL TESTING, GILL-NET FISHING, REDWOOD CHOPPING OR OIL DERRICK CON-STRUCTION ALONG OUR FOR-MERLY PRISTINE BEACHES??

DO ANY MEMBERS OF THE BOARD OF DIRECTORS' FAMI-LIES STILL USE PLASTIC FORKS AND/OR DISPOS-ABLE DIAPERS??!

THERE'S A GIFT WITH PURCHASE.

WRAP IT UP.

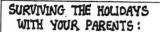

SURVIVING THE HOLIDAYS WITH YOUR PARENTS :
* Do not become defensive.
* Do not be overly critical.

* Respect your parents for the unique individuals they are.
* Make every moment together a memory to cherish for a lifetime.

YOU'RE GOING TO GROW A BIG HUMP ON YOUR BACK IF YOU SIT SLOUCHED OVER LIKE THAT, SWEETIE.

MAYBE I **WANT** A HUMP ON MY BACK !!

MOTHER : 649
MAGAZINE ARTICLES : ZILCH

smack!

HERE, CATHY, LET ME TAKE YOUR PICTURE !

NO...WAIT... I'LL TAKE **YOUR** PICTURE, MOM !

I'LL TAKE YOUR PICTURE TAKING MY PICTURE !

WAIT...WAIT... I'LL VIDEO YOU TAKING A PICTURE OF CATHY TAKING YOUR PICTURE !

ON THE COUNT OF THREE, WE WILL ALL SIMULTANEOUSLY POINT THE CAMERAS AT EACH OTHER AND SHOOT !

DON'T LOOK NOW, BUT IT'S THE ANNUAL CHRISTMAS ROLL FROM THE "CAMERA-FACE FAMILY."

HOUR PHOTO

OOF... I'M SO FULL... I CAN'T MOVE, MOM...

REALLY ?? THEN THIS MIGHT BE A GOOD TIME TO BROWSE THROUGH THE CHRISTMAS CARDS I RECEIVED FROM MOTHERS OF YOUR EX-BOYFRIENDS !

HUH ?...

WE'VE ALWAYS KEPT UP THE CORRESPONDENCE IN CASE THERE WERE ANY SPARKS TO BE REKINDLED !

YOU WHA...??

EACH CARD INCLUDES A PHOTO OF THE SON AND A SYNOPSIS OF HIS REACTION TO THE LITTLE VIDEO I SENT OF YOU.

Dear Martha,
   Cathy's eyes widened in disbelief when she saw the picture of your handsome Albert....

Panel 1: I NEED TO CALL THE OFFICE, MOM. / THE OFFICE! WAIT! LET ME MOVE THE PRINCESS PHONE INTO YOUR OWN LITTLE BEDROOM!

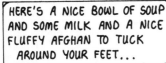

Panel 2: HERE'S A NICE BOWL OF SOUP AND SOME MILK AND A NICE FLUFFY AFGHAN TO TUCK AROUND YOUR FEET...

Panel 3: ....AND HERE'S A LITTLE BELL TO RING IF YOU NEED DAD OR ME TO RUSH BACK IN AND BRING YOU ANYTHING! / TUCK TUCK

Panel 4: THE TEENSY-WEENSY PART OF ME THAT DOESN'T HATE THIS WANTS SOME CHOCOLATE IN MY MILK. / 'BING!'

Panel 5: YOUR FATHER WOULD LOVE THIS! / GREAT. GET IT, MOM. / THAT?? YOU'RE BUYING THAT?? / SALE SALE

Panel 6: YOU FOUND THE ONE THING IN A 500-ACRE MALL THAT'S NOT ON SALE AND YOU'RE BUYING IT??!! / SALE

Panel 7: ALERT THE MEDIA! THEY'RE PAYING RETAIL!!! FOR THE FIRST TIME IN SIX MONTHS, SOMEONE'S PAYING RETAIL!! / SALE SALE

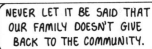

Panel 8: NEVER LET IT BE SAID THAT OUR FAMILY DOESN'T GIVE BACK TO THE COMMUNITY. / SALE / "CLAP" "CLAP CLAP"

Panel 9: UH, OH! I THINK SOMEONE WANTS TO GO OUT AGAIN! / MOM, PLEASE. I DON'T WANT HER GETTING USED TO GOING OUT EVERY TEN MINUTES. / YAP YAP YAP YAP

Panel 10: I TOOK HER THE LAST FOUR TIMES... GRANDPA TOOK HER TWICE BEFORE THAT, AND NOW I THINK SHE WANTS HER MOMMY! / I CAN'T TAKE HER OUT EVERY TEN MINUTES WHEN I WORK ALL DAY! / YAP YAP

Panel 11: SHE LOVES HER WALKS WITH MOMMY, DOESN'T SHE? / "MOMMY" SPENT THE LAST YEAR GETTING HER ON A SCHEDULE WHICH YOU HAVE DESTROYED IN THREE DAYS!! / YAP YAP YAP

Panel 12: AT LEAST WE KNOW SHE'LL THINK OF US AFTER SHE GOES HOME....

WHICH WOULD I RATHER DO? STARVE ALL DAY AND WEAR A GREAT NEW YEAR'S EVE DRESS TONIGHT...OR ENJOY MYSELF AND WEAR A PLATE OF COOKIES FOR THE NEXT TWO MONTHS?

EAT NOTHING AND POSSIBLY LOOK RAVISHING FOR FOUR HOURS...OR EAT EVERYTHING AND DOOM MYSELF TO EIGHT WEEKS OF SELF-TORTURE?

EVEN WHEN I KNOW THE PITFALLS, IT'S HARD NOT TO GO WITH THE LONG-TERM RELATIONSHIP.

GOOD MORNING AND WELCOME BACK. TODAY WILL BE DEVOTED TO A DISCUSSION OF WHAT WE GOT AND WHERE WE WENT FOR THE HOLIDAYS, INCLUDING A FULL ACCOUNTING OF AIRPORT HORROR STORIES, HIGHWAY PILEUPS AND PSYCHOTIC RELATIVES.

TOMORROW WE'LL DIVIDE INTO SMALL GROUPS TO ANALYZE OUR IMMATURE BEHAVIOR WITH OUR PARENTS, AND TO GIVE SPEECHES ON HOW OUR OWN SIX-MONTH RELATIONSHIPS ARE SUPERIOR IN EVERY WAY TO THEIR PATHETIC 40-YEAR MARRIAGES.

FRIDAY WE WILL WANDER THE HALLS ON OUR OWN, MOANING ABOUT THE DIETS, EXERCISE PLANS, BUDGETS AND ORGANIZATION SYSTEMS WE BLEW TEN MINUTES INTO THE NEW YEAR.

I CAN'T BELIEVE THIS, CATHY!

I KNOW. IT'S A LOT TO CRAM INTO A THREE-DAY WEEK.

53

ATTENTION ALL EMPLOYEES: THIS IS A NEW YEAR! A CLEAN SLATE! A FRESH START!

1991

I WANT 1990 PAPERS OFF YOUR DESKS... 1990 MEMOS OFF YOUR WALLS... 1990 FILES OUT OF YOUR FILES!

1991

BEFORE THIS DAY IS OVER, I WANT 1990 PUT TO BED!!

1990'S IN BED, BUT 1985, '86, '87, '88 AND '89 KEEP THRASHING AROUND AND PULLING ITS COVERS OFF.

I WILL TAKE EVERY NEUROTIC LITTLE PILE ON MY DESK, MIX THEM ALL TOGETHER, AND HEAP THEM IN THE TRASH!

I'LL SNEAK IN AT NIGHT, EMPTY THE FILE CABINETS AND DRIVE THE CONTENTS TO THE DUMPSTER!

I WILL HAVE A BONFIRE OF MY "TO READ" STACK! HA, HA! A CLEAN OFFICE! I WILL BE REBORN!! I WILL FINALLY BE ABLE TO BREATHE!!!

YOU HAVE TO SEPARATE EVERYTHING OUT FOR THE RECYCLERS FIRST, CATHY.

GLOBAL DESTRUCTION RUINS ANOTHER PARTY...

WHERE'S THE NEW, 1991 "COFFEE ROOM CLEANUP RULES" SIGN?

IT WAS DEFACED 15 MINUTES AFTER IT WAS PUT UP, MR. PINKLEY.

THE MEMO **CONCERNING** THE DEFACING OF THE "COFFEE ROOM CLEANUP RULES" SIGN WAS THEN SCANNED INTO THE COMPUTER, EMBELLISHED WITH LEWD CLIP ART, AND REDISTRIBUTED THROUGH THE DEPARTMENT.

THE ONE EMBELLISHED COPY THAT WAS NOT TURNED INTO A DART BOARD IS BEING SIMULTANEOUSLY FAXED TO 243 OFFICES AROUND THE GLOBE.

ONE WEEK INTO THE NEW YEAR, AND MY COMPANY'S ALREADY GONE WORLDWIDE.

FLATTERY

...COME ON, MY BEAUTIFUL CAR, START! MY SHINING, POWERFUL MACHINE... START!

BRIBERY

START AND I'LL GET YOU WASHED! START AND I'LL HAVE YOU VACUUMED! START AND I'LL CHANGE THE OIL!

HONESTY

START, YOU MISERABLE, GAS-GUZZLING JUNK HEAP!!!

DESPITE A FULL RANGE OF COMMUNICATION SKILLS, ANOTHER RELATIONSHIP GOES NOWHERE.

OH, IRVING, MY CAR WON'T START AND I HAVE TO GET TO WORK AND I DON'T KNOW WHAT TO DO! PLEASE RESCUE ME!!

HE'LL COMFORT ME OVER BREAKFAST...BUT I DON'T HAVE ANY FOOD. I HAVE TO GET TO THE STORE FOR FOOD. I CAN'T GET TO THE STORE BECAUSE MY CAR WON'T START...

CALL A CAB! TAKE THE BUS! RUN THROUGH THE BLIZZARD ON MY OWN TWO LEGS!! I MUST GET FOOD AND BE BACK HOME IN 15 MINUTES!!!

...AMAZING HOW INVINCIBLE I GET WHEN I'M PREPARING TO BE TOTALLY HELPLESS...

IRVING WILL RUSH IN...CUP MY LITTLE FACE IN HIS STRONG HANDS...HE'LL SAY I LOOK BEAUTIFUL WITH SNOW STILL GLISTENING IN MY HAIR... I'LL TELL HIM HE'S MY HERO....

WE'LL SNUGGLE IN THE KITCHEN WITH HOT COFFEE AND STEAMY ROLLS...TRYING TO MAKE A PLAN ...SLOWLY FORGETTING ALL ABOUT THE CAR THAT WON'T START... FORGETTING EVERYTHING BUT....

HI. I CALLED A TOW TRUCK, CATHY. HE'LL BE HERE IN TEN MINUTES. GOT TO GO. I'M LATE.

MEN HAVE NO CONCEPT OF HOW TO HANDLE A CRISIS.

58

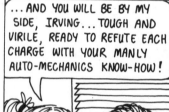

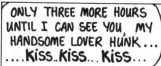

65

66

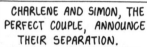

I BROUGHT HOME FOUR REPORTS TO WRITE. DIDN'T TOUCH THEM.

I BROUGHT HOME THREE POUNDS OF READING MATERIAL. DIDN'T GLANCE AT IT.

I BROUGHT HOME ONE TEENSY QUESTION ABOUT MY RELATIONSHIP. **IT** FILLED UP MY WHOLE HOUSE, CONTAMINATED EVERY SPECK OF AIR, PLASTERED ITSELF ALL OVER EVERY SURFACE AND MUTILATED MY EVENING.

IF ONLY BRAINS COULD BE STUFFED INTO BRIEFCASES SO WE'D NEVER BE TEMPTED TO LOOK AT THEM...

WE'RE HAPPY, AREN'T WE, IRVING?

OF COURSE WE'RE HAPPY, CATHY.

THERE'S THIS BREAK-UP VIRUS GOING AROUND THE OFFICE, AND I JUST NEED TO MAKE SURE WE'RE REALLY HAPPY.

WE'RE REALLY HAPPY.

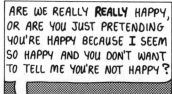

ARE WE REALLY **REALLY** HAPPY, OR ARE YOU JUST PRETENDING YOU'RE HAPPY BECAUSE I SEEM SO HAPPY AND YOU DON'T WANT TO TELL ME YOU'RE NOT HAPPY?

...AACK!! PARANOIA!! THE FIRST SYMPTOM!

WHY DID YOU ASK? AREN'T YOU REALLY HAPPY?

HI, SWEETIE. IT'S MOM. HOW WAS YOUR WEEK?

FINE.

UH, OH. WHEN YOU SAY IT WAS FINE, IT MEANS YOU'RE NOT TALKING, SO I HAVE TO ASSUME IT WAS TERRIBLE.

I ONLY KNOW YOUR WEEK WAS OKAY IF YOU SAY IT WAS AWFUL, BECAUSE THEN I KNOW YOU'VE COPED WITH IT, GOTTEN OVER IT, AND AREN'T TRYING TO KEEP ANYTHING FROM YOUR MOTHER.

OKAY! MY WEEK WAS AWFUL, MOM!

OH, POOR BABY! I'LL BE RIGHT OVER!!

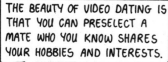

THE BEAUTY OF VIDEO DATING IS THAT YOU CAN PRESELECT A MATE WHO YOU KNOW SHARES YOUR HOBBIES AND INTERESTS.

VIDEO ♥ MATE

SIGN UP!

WE HAVE THE SPORTY TYPE...
THE ARTY TYPE...
THE BRAINY TYPE...
THE CUDDLY TYPE...
JUST TELL US WHAT YOU WANT!

SPORTY

ARTY

I WANT TO GET BACK AT THE MAN WHO RUINED MY LIFE !!!

AH! OUR BIGGEST CATEGORY! THE REVENGE-Y TYPE!

REVENGEY

BR

FEEL FREE TO STOP IN THE LADIES ROOM WHILE WE SET UP TO MAKE YOUR VIDEO-TAPE, CHARLENE.

NO, THANKS. THIS IS HOW I AM! TAKE IT OR LEAVE IT!

VIDEO ♥ MATE

...WELL, MAYBE JUST A DAB OF LIPSTICK. BUT THAT'S IT. NO CAMOUFLAGE! NO HOCUS-POCUS!

DIES

...OKAY, MAYBE JUST A TEENSY BIT OF CONCEALER... MAYBE JUST A TOUCH OF BLUSH...A LITTLE EYELINER....

...AND GEL! I NEED GEL!! BRING ME GEL AND A STYLING WAND!!

JUST POINT THE CAMERA AT THE DOOR. IT'S ALL ANY MAN WILL EVER SEE OF HER ANYWAY.

LADIES

JUST RELAX AND TALK ABOUT WHAT YOU'RE LOOKING FOR IN A RELA-TIONSHIP.

I DON'T WANT TO SOUND TOO AVAILABLE.

VIDEO MATE

THIS IS A VIDEO DATING SER-VICE, CHARLENE. YOU'RE SUP-POSED TO SOUND AVAILABLE.

HI! MY NAME IS CHARLENE. YOU CAN'T HAVE ME! DON'T EVEN TRY! I'M ALREADY IN-VOLVED! OFF THE MARKET! LEAVE ME ALONE !!!

VIDEO MATE

CUT!

SORRY. FORCE OF HABIT.

THE CAMERA-MAN WANTS YOUR PHONE NUMBER.

WE HAVE MANY EAGER, YOUNG PROFESSIONAL MEN...

OH, NO. NO "YUPPIES"!

WE HAVE LOTS OF OLDER DIVORCÉS...

OH, NO. NO "MID-LIFE CRISES"!

NO "BURNED-OUT LAWYERS"! NO "AGING JOCKS"! NO "FORMER-STOCKBROKERS-TURNED-ORGANIC-FRUIT-FARMERS"!

I KNOW, I KNOW...THE "OVERLY-PICKY-BIOLOGICAL-CLOCKERS" NEVER WANT TO DATE CLICHÉS.

YOU'RE NOT LOOKING AT ANY OF THE MEN I PICKED OUT FOR YOU.

IT JUST SEEMS SO PERSONAL. WOULDN'T THEY BE EMBARRASSED TO KNOW I WAS WATCHING THEIR TAPES?

CATHY, ALL THOSE MEN SIGNED UP HOPING THEY'D MEET A WOMAN AS SENSITIVE AND CARING AS YOU...HERE. I'LL CLOSE THE DOOR SO YOU CAN GIVE THEM THE PRIVACY AND RESPECT YOU TREASURE SO HIGHLY.

VIDEO♥MATE VIEWING ROOM

...AND I LOVE A TIDY SOCK DRAWER...

COME IN HERE, CHARLENE! GET A LOAD OF THIS ONE!!

CHARLENE FORCED ME TO GO TO THE VIDEO-DATING PLACE WITH HER, AND SOMEHOW I WOUND UP HAVING A TAPE MADE OF MYSELF, ELECTRA!

OF COURSE, I DIDN'T MAKE THE TAPE ON PURPOSE... I WAS JUST SHOWING HER HOW TO DO IT, AND THEY ACCIDENTALLY MADE ONE OF ME!

IT'S NOTHING I WOULD EVER REALLY DO... OKAY, I DID IT... BUT JUST BY ACCIDENT, SO EVEN THOUGH I WENT AHEAD AND SIGNED UP, IT ISN'T AS THOUGH I'M REALLY...HA...HA...

WE KNOW WE'RE IN TROUBLE WHEN IT DOESN'T EVEN SOUND GOOD BEING EXPLAINED TO A DOG.

THINGS TO NEVER TRY EXPLAINING TO A MAN:

1. WHY SOCIAL EVENTS HAVE TO BE CANCELED FOR SIX WEEKS IF YOUR BANGS GET CUT 1/8 INCH TOO SHORT.

2. THE EFFECT THAT ONE FLUORESCENT LIGHT IN A DRESSING ROOM CAN HAVE ON ALL FUTURE PHYSICAL ACTIVITY WITH HIM.

3. THE DIFFERENCE BETWEEN THE NINE SHADES OF TAUPE EYESHADOW IN YOUR BATHROOM.

4. THE DIFFERENCE BETWEEN THE 16 PAIRS OF BLACK SHOES IN YOUR CLOSET.

5. THE DIFFERENCE BETWEEN TAKING 25 BITES OF HIS PIE VS. ORDERING ONE OF YOUR OWN.

YOU SIGNED UP FOR VIDEO DATING?!

IT WAS JUST FOR FUN... JUST FOR LAUGHS.. ..HA...HA....

6. ANY IDEA EVER SUGGESTED BY A SINGLE GIRLFRIEND.

I TOLD IRVING I SIGNED UP FOR VIDEO DATING AND NOW HE ISN'T SPEAKING TO ME, CHARLENE. I HOPE YOU'RE HAPPY.

I AM! I TOLD SIMON I SIGNED UP FOR VIDEO DATING AND HE BEGGED ME TO COME BACK TO HIM, SO I CANCELED MY MEMBERSHIP!!

YOU CANCELED?? YOU DRAGGED ME INTO THIS, DESTROYED MY RELATIONSHIP, AND NOW YOU'RE LEAVING ME ALL ALONE?!!

OH, YOU WON'T BE ALONE, CATHY.

VIDEO-MATE ALREADY CALLED AND HAS FOUR LIVE ONES WHO ARE PANTING TO MEET YOU!

HI. I'M ROD. I'VE GOT THE PORSCHE WITH A PHONE, THE PAD WITH A VIEW... NOW ALL I NEED IS A CLASSY LADY LIKE YOU!

AACK!

HI. I'M CARL. I'M INTO FEELINGS. YOUR FEELINGS. MY FEELINGS. OUR FEELINGS. YOUR FEELINGS ABOUT OUR FEELINGS. MY FEELINGS ABOUT...

AACK!!

HI. I'M BERNIE.

AAACK!!

BAM BAM

HI. I'M CATHY. I WANT MY MONEY BACK.

THESE WERE NOT THE MEN I PICKED! WHERE ARE THE MEN I PICKED??

NONE OF THE MEN YOU PICKED PICKED YOU.

THE MEN I PICKED CAME IN, LOOKED AT MY TAPE AND DIDN'T PICK ME??

THE SAME MEN WHO WERE "SEARCHING FOR A WOMAN OF DEPTH AND SENSITIVITY" REJECTED ME ON THE BASIS OF A THREE-MINUTE VIDEOTAPE??

YOU DIDN'T EVEN LOOK AT THIS ONE, CATHY.

I DON'T LIKE THE WAY HIS NAME IS TYPED ON THE BOX.

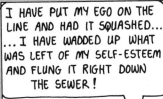

IS IT WORSE TO MEET HIM IN A RESTAURANT AND HAVE A ROOMFUL OF TOTAL STRANGERS STARING AT US DURING OUR "GETTING TO KNOW YOU" MEAL...

OR IS IT WORSE TO MEET HIM IN THE PRIVACY OF MY HOME AND HAVE A POTENTIAL PSYCHO-PATH KNOW WHERE I LIVE?

EMBARRASSMENT OR DEATH. ALWAYS A TOUGH CALL, CATHY.

EVEN WHEN I KNOW WHO I'M GOING TO BE WITH, THERE'S NO DECENT WAY TO MEET A MAN!!!

I ACCEPTED A DATE WITH A MAN I KNOW NOTHING ABOUT EX-CEPT WHAT I SAW ON HIS THREE-MINUTE "VIDEO-MATE" TAPE, MOTHER.

HAVE A NICE TIME, DEAR.

"HAVE A NICE TIME"?? THAT'S IT?

CATHY, YOUR FATHER AND I SUPPORT YOU IN THIS JUST AS WE SUPPORT YOU IN ALL THINGS.

NO MATTER WHAT YOU DO OR WHERE YOU GO, WE ARE ALWAYS HERE FOR YOU!

...QUIETLY RIPPING OUR HAIR OUT.

WHEW, BOY! I HATE FIRST DATES!

I HATE PEOPLE WHO SAY THEY HATE FIRST DATES ON THE FIRST DATE.

I HATE THE AWKWARDNESS... HATE THE FORMALITY...

I HATE HAVING THE SAME STUPID CONVERSATION.

I HATE THAT WHOLE "TRYING-TO-GUESS-IF-IT'S-GOING-ANYWHERE" THING.

I HATE THIS RESTAURANT. I HATE HIM. I HATE MYSELF.

BRING THE MENUS! LET'S GET THIS OVER WITH!!

I HATE FIRST DATES...

80

81

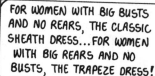

82

I COULD WEAR THIS, BUT I'D HAVE TO IRON THE BLOUSE THAT GOES WITH IT...

I AM NOT IRONING A BLOUSE TODAY! I DON'T HAVE TIME TO IRON A BLOUSE TODAY!!

I DON'T CARE IF I HAVE TO TRY ON EVERY STUPID THING IN THIS CLOSET! I AM NOT GOING TO WASTE FIVE MINUTES OF MY VALUABLE TIME IRONING A BLOUSE!!!

CATHY'S RUNNING A FEW HOURS LATE, MR. PINKLEY... SHE'S SPENDING THE MORNING NOT IRONING ANYTHING.

RECEPTIONIST

TO LOOK "OFFICE ACCEPTABLE" A MAN NEEDS A $200 SUIT, $60 SHOES, A $30 SHIRT, $5 OF UNDERWEAR AND A $10 HAIRCUT.

ACCOUNTANT

TO LOOK "OFFICE ACCEPTABLE," A WOMAN NEEDS A $200 SUIT, $80 SHOES, A $90 BLOUSE, $35 OF LINGERIE, A $45 HAIRCUT, $5 PANTYHOSE, $46 OF MAKEUP, A $10 MANICURE, $200 OF JEWELRY, AND A $30 PURSE CONTAINING $9 OF EMERGENCY SUPPLIES TO MAINTAIN HER "PROFESSIONAL LOOK" THROUGHOUT THE DAY.

WOMEN

THUS, ON BEHALF OF ALL WOMEN, I DEMAND A YEAR-END REFUND FOR EACH OF US, PLUS $10 PER HOUR FOR ALL THE EXTRA SHOPPING TIME REQUIRED!

IT ALL EVENS OUT WITH THE EXTRA ASPIRIN MEN HAVE TO BUY.

MEDICINE IS A DIFFERENT CATEGORY. SHALL I BEGIN WITH OUR THERAPY BILLS?...

ACCOUNTANT

MEDICINE
MEN
WOMEN

JANUARY, 1990: $425 THROWN AWAY ON WORKOUT EQUIPMENT I DIDN'T USE...

MARCH, 1990: $250 THROWN AWAY ON SHOES I DIDN'T NEED...

TAX STUFF

MAY, 1990: $68 THROWN AWAY ON PLANTS I MURDERED...

JULY, 1990: $133 THROWN AWAY ON SELF-IMPROVEMENT BOOKS I DIDN'T READ...

TAX STUFF

SEPTEMBER, 1990: $85 THROWN AWAY ON A HAIRDO I HATED...

NOVEMBER, 1990: $100 THROWN AWAY ON FOOD I THREW AWAY...

TAX STUFF

A DECADE OF FINANCIAL INDEPENDENCE, AND THE ONLY CONCEPT I'VE TRULY MASTERED IS THAT OF "DISPOSABLE INCOME."

TAX STUFF

85

MONEY MAGAZINE HAD 49 DIFFERENT TAX PREPARERS DO THE SAME TAX RETURN AND THEY GOT 49 DIFFERENT ANSWERS... ...RANGING FROM A TAX DUE OF $6,807 TO $73,247!!

HOW DO I KNOW YOU'RE NOT ALL JUST GUESSING?? HOW DO I KNOW SOMEONE ELSE WOULDN'T HAVE GUESSED LOWER??

PLEASE...GIVE ME A SHRED OF REASSURANCE... TELL ME SOMETHING TO MAKE ME FEEL BETTER!

IF YOU POP YOUR RETURN IN THE MAIL RIGHT NOW, YOU WON'T HAVE TO THINK ABOUT IT FOR A YEAR.

AH.

OH, HOW THE WORLD LOVES AN HONEST ACCOUNTANT....

ACCOUNTANT

MY TAXES WIPED ME OUT! WHAT AM I GOING TO DO??

ACCEPT THE FACT THAT YOU'RE WALLOWING IN THE WASTELAND OF YOUR OWN MAKING AND MOVE ON, MR. PINKLEY!

HUH?

TODAY IS A NEW DAY! EVERY MOMENT YOU DON'T BLOW IT AS BADLY AS YOU BLEW IT BEFORE IS A VICTORY!

IF YOU'VE EVEN MADE IT TO 9:00 THIS MORNING WITHOUT ANY OF YOUR USUAL BLUNDERS, YOU'VE SCORED A RICH, PERSONAL TRIUMPH! A BUILDING BLOCK TOWARD THE NEW YOU!

...UH, THANKS, CATHY...

IF 15 YEARS OF DIETING HAVE TAUGHT ME ANYTHING, IT'S HOW TO START OVER.

WHO WILL STAY LATE TO FINISH THIS?

I HAVE TO PICK UP JOSH AT PRE-SCHOOL.

I HAVE TO TAKE JENNY TO BALLET.

I HAVE TO CARPOOL JAKE'S LITTLE LEAGUE.

I HAVE TO MAKE DINNER FOR JULIE.

I HAVE TO MEET SOMEONE, FALL IN LOVE, GET MARRIED, SET UP HOUSE, GET PREGNANT AND GIVE BIRTH!!!

HAVE IT ON MY DESK BY MORNING, CATHY.

IF PARENTS CAN LEAVE AT 5:00, SINGLE PEOPLE SHOULD GET TO GO HOME AT NOON.

I CALLED IRVING 4.6 MORE TIMES THAN HE CALLED ME LAST MONTH. FOR EACH TIME I GOT HIS VOICE-MAIL, I GET TWO EXTRA POINTS. FOR EACH EMOTIONALLY RISKY EVENING CALL, EIGHT EXTRA POINTS.

MEANWHILE, I STAGED SEVEN "RELATIONSHIP EPISODES," WHICH WERE THREE TIMES WORSE THAN THE TWO HE STAGED... WHICH WOULD MAKE US EVEN EXCEPT THE LAST ONE WAS AT HIS HOUSE, GIVING ME NINE BONUS POINTS FOR DRIVING OVER!

THEREFORE, I WIN! IT IS HIS TURN TO CALL!!

CATHY, HE ISN'T GOING TO KNOW THAT.

IGNORANCE OF THE RULES! TWO DEMERITS! THE NEXT FIVE CALLS ARE HIS!!

MR. PINKLEY! THE FLOWERS YOU SENT ME FOR SECRETARIES WEEK ARE GORGEOUS!

THE WHAT? ...AHEM... I WHAT??

LOOK AT THIS ARRANGEMENT! IT MUST HAVE COST A FORTUNE!

...WELL... AHEM.... NOTHING'S TOO GOOD FOR MY SECRETARY.

...AND THE LITTLE CARD YOU ENCLOSED PROMISING ME STOCK OPTIONS AND A BRAND-NEW, BRIGHT-RED MIATA WAS SUCH A SWEET TOUCH!

THUNK!

WHAT DO YOU BET HE'LL RE-MEMBER TO SEND THEM HIMSELF NEXT YEAR?

WILL I GET A FREE PARKING SPOT WITH THIS?

SECRETARIES WORK LIKE MANI-ACS FOR DEADLINES WE CAN'T CHANGE... POLICIES WE CAN'T ALTER... CO-WORKERS WE CAN'T CHOOSE... CLIENTS WE CAN'T YELL AT AND MEETINGS WE CAN'T GO TO!

Secretaries Week

IN SHORT, WE HAVE ALL THE PRESSURES OF BUSINESS WITH NONE OF THE POWER, MAKING OURS THE HIGHEST-STRESS JOB IN THE OFFICE!

OH YEAH?? TRY MY JOB!!

Secretaries Week

...AND THE FINAL TORTURE, A DOOR WE CAN'T CLOSE.

Secretaries Week

89

Panel 1: WE BROUGHT DOUGHNUTS FOR SECRETARIES WEEK, CHARLENE, BUT SOMEONE TOOK BITES OUT OF ALL OF THEM BEFORE WE COULD BRING THEM TO YOU!

Panel 2: WE GOT YOU A CAKE, BUT THE WHOLE THING DISAPPEARED BY THE TIME WE ROUNDED UP ENOUGH NON-PLASTIC FORKS!

Panel 3: WE'D TOAST YOU WITH COFFEE, BUT SOMEONE DIDN'T TURN OFF THE POT LAST NIGHT AND THERE'S A HALF-INCH OF CRUD WELDED TO THE BOTTOM!

Panel 4: BESIDES, THE MUGS ARE ALL FILTHY BECAUSE SOMEONE DIDN'T TAKE HIS TURN AT KITCHEN DUTY!!!

NEVER LET IT BE SAID THIS OFFICE DOESN'T KNOW HOW TO PARTY.

Panel 5: BINKMAN NEEDED THIS ASAP!

I SENT A COPY FOR OVERNIGHT DELIVERY. HE'LL HAVE IT IN THE MORNING.

Panel 6: OVERNIGHT?? WHAT IS THIS, THE STONE AGE?!

Panel 7: WE HAVE A $5,000 ELECTRONIC TRANSMITTAL SYSTEM, AND YOU CAN'T GET IT WHERE IT NEEDS TO GO FASTER THAN OVERNIGHT??!!

Panel 8: CALL ME A ROMANTIC...I STILL BELIEVE IN THE POWER OF THE PRINTED PAGE....

Panel 9: HEY, THERE...DON'T I KNOW YOU?

ME? NO. I DON'T THINK SO.

Panel 10: YOU LOOK SO FAMILIAR. HAVE YOU EVER BEEN ON TV?

TV?? NO. NO TV! NO! NEVER!

Panel 11: YES YOU HAVE...YOU'RE...YOU'RE... VIDEO-DATE #4327!! "LOVES HOLDING HANDS IN THE MOONLIGHT"!!!

Panel 12: HE SIGNED UP, TOO, OR HE WOULDN'T KNOW!

I HAVE A SINGLE NEPHEW IF YOU'RE REALLY THAT DESPERATE.

THE COUCH IS WHERE DIETS DIE, ELECTRA! WE ARE NOT GOING NEAR THAT COUCH TONIGHT!!

CLICK

IF THE COUCH IS WHERE DIETS DIE, THE BED IS WHERE THEY GO TO GET BURIED....

CLICK

COOKIES

6:00PM: RACE OUT OF OFFICE. DRIVE AS FAST AS POSSIBLE TO GYM BEFORE ALL PARKING SPACES ARE GONE...

CIRCLE LOT 17 TIMES...PARK HALF A MILE AWAY...RUN TO GYM...

FLING SELF INTO WORKOUT CLOTHES BEFORE LINES FORM FOR ALL GOOD MACHINES...

PACE BETWEEN MACHINES... GIVE UP AND JOIN ADVANCED "STEP CLASS" HALF-WAY IN THE MIDDLE...

ZOOM HOME. WALK AND FEED DOG. SHOWER. WASH AND DRY HAIR. REDO CONTACTS. REDO MAKEUP. FIND, IRON AND PUT ON KICKY, CASUAL EVENING OUTFIT...

HI, IRVING! I'M HOME! WANT TO GO SEE A MOVIE TONIGHT?

IT'S 11:30, CATHY. I'M ALREADY IN BED.

PANT PANT

THUS CONCLUDES THE FIRST AND LAST DAY OF THE "AFTER-WORK WORKOUT" PROGRAM.

YES!! THE JEANS ARE ZIPPED!!

I COULDN'T GET THESE JEANS OVER MY HIPS LAST WEEK, AND NOW THEY'RE ZIPPED! I CAN LIVE AGAIN!! I CAN LOVE! I CAN FROLIC!!

STAND BACK, WORLD! HERE I COME!!

HOP HOP HOP

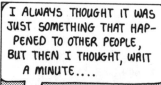

THE BIG NEWS IN SWIMWEAR THIS YEAR IS THE BUST!

I'M OUT OF HERE.

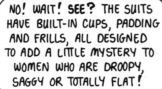

NO! WAIT! SEE? THE SUITS HAVE BUILT-IN CUPS, PADDING AND FRILLS, ALL DESIGNED TO ADD A LITTLE MYSTERY TO WOMEN WHO ARE DROOPY, SAGGY OR TOTALLY FLAT!

IF EVERYONE KNOWS THESE ARE FOR WOMEN WHO ARE DROOPY, SAGGY OR FLAT, THERE IS NO MYSTERY!

CERTAINLY THERE'S MYSTERY.

THEY DON'T KNOW WHICH ONE OF THOSE YOU ARE, NOW, DO THEY??

I'M OUT OF HERE.

IN YET ANOTHER ASTOUNDING DISPLAY OF EMPATHY FOR THEIR LESS-THAN-WELL-ENDOWED CUSTOMERS, THE SWIMWEAR INDUSTRY HAS BROUGHT BACK A CLASSIC LINE FROM 1955......

4   5   6

"DON'T LIE ON YOUR STOMACH ON CEMENT."

THE LEGS ARE CUT TOO HIGH! THE COLOR IS NAUSEATING! THE "BUST" IS TWO INCHES ABOVE MY WAIST IF THE BACK'S PULLED DOWN FAR ENOUGH TO COVER MY REAR!

THE TRIPLE-REINFORCED, CRISS-CROSSED "TUMMY CONTROL PANEL" SQUASHES ME LIKE A SCREAMING GREEN SAUSAGE!!!

....AMAZING HOW THEY SETTLE DOWN WHEN YOU FIND A SUIT THAT COVERS THE MAIN FIGURE PROBLEM AREA.

YOU CAN HAVE RUFFLES ON THE TOP AND TRY TO LOOK AS THOUGH YOU DON'T HAVE A TEENY CHEST...

OR YOU CAN HAVE RUFFLES ON THE BOTTOM AND TRY TO LOOK AS THOUGH YOU DON'T HAVE A BIG REAR...

OR YOU CAN HAVE RUFFLES **BOTH** PLACES AND HOPE EVERYONE WILL GET THE RUFFLES CONFUSED AND START THINKING YOU'RE TRYING TO CONCEAL A CHEST THAT'S TOO BIG AND A REAR THAT'S TOO TEENY!

BINGO!

EXCELLENT CHOICE. WHY JUST FOOL THE MEN WHEN THERE'S A CHANCE WE CAN ALSO DELUDE OURSELVES?

☼ BEACHWEAR EVOLUTION ☼
1951: THE TWO-PIECE

1971: THE ONE-PIECE

1991: THE 36-PIECE

SPF 36
SPF 25
SPF 42
SPF 15
SPF 98

GLOVES! I NEED GLOVES! MY FINGERS MIGHT BE SHOWING!

OF THE 250,000 WORDS IN THE ENGLISH LANGUAGE, AND THE 25 ZILLION POSSIBLE COMBINATIONS, ALMOST NONE WILL HAVE THE IMPACT ON A WOMAN'S LIFE AS THIS ONE LITTLE OFF-HAND REMARK...

OH, HA, HA! WHAT THE HECK? LET'S TRY SOMETHING DIFFERENT TODAY!

MARGO: ASKED FOR A NEW LOOK. GOT A NEW LOOK.

RUTH: ASKED FOR A NEW LOOK. GOT A NEW LOOK.

KIM: ASKED FOR A NEW LOOK. GOT A NEW LOOK.

CATHY: ASKED FOR A NEW LOOK. GOT A NEW LOOK.

CATHY'S AT HOME WITH A FAMILY EMERGENCY.

A FAMILY EMERGENCY?

IS SHE OK? ARE HER PARENTS OK??

CATHY! WHAT HAPPENED?? MR. PINKLEY SAID YOU HAD A FAMILY EMERGENCY!!

THE EVIL TWIN THAT LIVES INSIDE MY BRAIN WANTED TO TRY "HIGHLIGHTS AND A BODY PERM"!!!

...NO...TELL ME I DIDN'T HAVE ANYTHING DONE TO MY HAIR... IT WAS JUST A NIGHTMARE... IT HAD TO BE A NIGHTMARE...

PLEASE LET IT BE A NIGHTMARE ...PLEASE DON'T LET MY HAIR BE A PLATINUM BLOND BUBBLE... PLEASE...PLEASE...PLEASE... PLEASE...   PLEASE....

AAACK!!

WITH A SICKENING BUT UNDENIABLE TWINGE OF PRIDE, SHE REALIZES SHE ACTUALLY MADE IT OUT OF BED WITHOUT DWELLING ON HER WEIGHT.

102

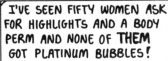

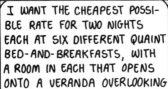

107

I'M LOOKING FOR A BREEZY YET CHIC LONG SUMMER DRESS IN A MINT GREEN WRINKLE-RESISTANT FABRIC FOR MY VACATION NEXT WEEK!

NEW FALL ARRIVALS
FALL
FALL FASHION

...OKAY, IT COULD BE PANTS AND A JACKET, BUT SUMMERY! CHIC AND SUMMERY!

NEW FALL ARRIVALS
FALL

...OKAY, IT COULD BE ANYTHING! ANYTHING FOR SUMMER! I HAVE TO HAVE SOME NEW SUMMERY THING FOR MY TRIP!!!

HOW ALL THE REALLY ICKY TANK TOPS FINALLY GET SOLD.

FALL FASHIONS
SUMMER SALE

NOT TONIGHT, IRVING. I HAVE TO TRY ON ALL MY CLOTHES FOR OUR TRIP!

YOU HAVE TO TRY ON YOUR OWN CLOTHES??
OF COURSE! I HAVE TO TRY THEM ON SO I'LL KNOW WHAT TO BRING.

CATHY, THEY'RE YOUR CLOTHES! JUST STICK THEM IN A SUITCASE!!
STICK CLOTHES IN A SUITCASE WITHOUT TRYING THEM ON?!

WOMEN DON'T KNOW HOW TO PACK!
MEN DON'T HAVE TO GUESS WHAT SIZE THEY'LL BE BY THE TIME THE PLANE LANDS.

HAIRDRYER
IRON
SHAMPOO
MOUSSE
GEL
CONDITIONER
CURLERS
SPRAY
MAKEUP
MOISTURIZER
CLEANSER
MASQUE
NAIL POLISH
POLISH REMOVER
HAND LOTION

TAPE PLAYER
BATTERIES
CASSETTES
CAMERA
FILM
CLOCK
DATEBOOK
ADDRESS BOOK
SEWING KIT
SNACKS
SUNSCREEN
HATS
PURSES
PANTYHOSE
SHOES

CLOTHES, JEWELRY, UMBRELLA, SUNGLASSES, PAPER, ENVELOPES, PENS, STAMPS, TAPE, FIRST AID KIT, CONTACT STUFF, FLASHLIGHT, BOOKS TO READ, NEWSPAPERS TO GO THROUGH, LETTERS TO ANSWER, PROJECTS TO THINK ABOUT, BILLS TO PAY, SAFETY PINS, TOOTHPASTE, DENTAL FLOSS, LINTBRUSH, SCISSORS, STAPLER...

SOME PEOPLE "GET AWAY FROM IT ALL". I JUST MOVE IT TO A NEW LOCATION.

I'M NOT REALLY HUNGRY.

I KNOW, IRVING... THE AIR PRESSURE IN THE CABIN MAKES YOUR CELLS EXPAND, CAUSING YOU TO FEEL FAT AND FULL.

OF COURSE, YOU HAVEN'T **REALLY** GAINED WEIGHT, BUT BECAUSE YOU **FEEL** AS IF YOU DID, IT'S COMMON TO EAT TOO MUCH OUT OF FRUSTRATION, STARTING A CHAIN REACTION OF OVEREATING THAT **GUARANTEES** YOU'LL GAIN WEIGHT BY THE END OF THE VACATION!

WHY WOULD I EAT IF I WEREN'T HUNGRY?

WHY DIDN'T I GO WITH A GIRL-FRIEND??

SHE SHOPPED. SHE PACKED. SHE SHOPPED. SHE PACKED.

SHE RE-SHOPPED, RE-PACKED... RE-SHOPPED, RE-PACKED... RE-SHOPPED, RE-PACKED...

...UNTIL FINALLY, EXHAUSTED AND READY TO RELAX WITH THE MAN SHE LOVES, SHE ARRIVES AT THE RESORT WITH ONLY ONE THING ON HER MIND...

IS THE GIFT STORE OPEN?

IT'S MIDNIGHT, MA'AM.

I GUESS THAT MEANS THE DRIVING RANGE IS OUT.

REGISTRATION

IT USED TO TAKE ME DAYS TO UNWIND ON VACATION, BUT NO MORE! I'M ALREADY STRESS-FREE, CATHY!

I WAS STRESS-FREE BEFORE THE PLANE LANDED!

Desert Café

I AM COMPLETELY RELAXED!

HAH! WELL, I AM **TOTALLY** RELAXED!

Desert Café

I'M MORE RELAXED THAN YOU ARE!!

I'M SO RELAXED I'M BARELY BREATHING!

HAH!

HAH!

THE PRINCE AND PRINCESS OF MELLOWNESS APPEAR TO BE READY TO ORDER.

Desert Café

112

DON'T LEAVE THE DOOR OPEN. YOU'LL LET ALL THE COLD AIR OUT! DON'T THROW YOUR TOWELS AROUND. WHAT WILL THE CLEANING PEOPLE THINK?!

DON'T GO OUTSIDE WITHOUT SUNSCREEN! DON'T FORGET YOUR TOOTHBRUSH SO YOU CAN BRUSH AFTER LUNCH!

DON'T DRINK COFFEE ON AN EMPTY STOMACH! DON'T USE BUTTER. IT WILL GO RIGHT TO YOUR THIGHS!

Dear Mother,
I'd write you a post-card about my vacation, except you seem to be on it with me.

ONE-WEEK VACATION... WITH HIM EVERY DAY... A THOUSAND EVENTS... NO ONE TO TELL...

NO WAY TO PROCESS IT... NO PERSPECTIVE... NO INTERPRETATIONS... NO REHASHES... NO COUNTERPOINT... NO PEP TALKS.....

AAACK!!

...CATHY?

SORRY, IRVING. GIRLFRIEND WITHDRAWAL.

MMM! THIS IS GREAT! I LOVE ICE CREAM!

ME TOO! I LOVE CHOCOLATE!

ME TOO! CHOCO-LATE'S THE BEST! LET'S HAVE MORE CHOCOLATE!

CHOCOLATE WITH CHOCOLATE SPRINKLES!

THIS IS PERFECT! GREAT IDEA! HA, HA, HA! WE'RE EXACTLY ALIKE!

WHEW! THAT WAS FUN! LET'S GO FOR A SWIM!

THE SIMILARI-TIES COME SCREECHING TO A HALT.

1ST DAY OF VACATION: LEISURELY DRIVE.

2ND – 6TH DAY OF VACATION: GOLF. SHOP.

LAST DAY OF VACATION: GOLF, SHOP, HORSEBACK RIDE, HIKE, FISH, SAIL, SWIM, READ, VOLLEYBALL, MOUNTAIN CLIMB, WATER SKI, HOT-AIR BALLOON, SNORKEL, TENNIS, TAKE PICTURES, TOUR MUSEUMS, TOUR GALLERIES, TOUR SITES, WRITE POSTCARDS, WRITE POSTCARDS, WRITE POSTCARDS

TRAINED BY YEARS IN BUSINESS, ANOTHER COUPLE HAS AN INVOLUNTARY RESPONSE TO A DEADLINE.

IT'S SO NICE HERE, CATHY. MAYBE WE SHOULD STAY AN EXTRA DAY.

WE CAN'T, IRVING! THE PLANE FARE WILL GO UP!

WE ALREADY PAID FULL COACH! I'LL JUST SEE WHAT THEY HAVE.

NO! DON'T CALL ATTENTION TO YOURSELF! THEY'LL LOOK UP YOUR RATE AND CHANGE IT!

THEY CAN'T CHANGE A FULL-FARE RATE!

PARDON THE RING! WRONG NUMBER! WE WEREN'T THINKING OF CHANGING ANYTHING! NO CHANGES!!

THEN AGAIN, WE'VE PROBABLY SPENT ENOUGH TIME TOGETHER...

WHAT IF THEY RECOGNIZED MY VOICE, BROUGHT UP OUR RECORD AND DUMPED IT ???

WE'RE LATE! WE'RE LATE!

THE SUITCASE WON'T CLOSE! THE SUITCASE WON'T CLOSE!

WHERE'S THE SHUTTLE BUS ?? WHERE'S THE SHUTTLE BUS ??

HURRY HURRY HURRY HURRY

GATES 150-156

NICE VACATION?

WHAT VACATION?!

DUE TO HEAVY TRAFFIC, WE'LL BE SITTING ON THE RUNWAY FOR THE NEXT TWO HOURS.

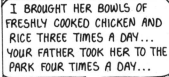

Panel 1:
WAS ELECTRA ANY TROUBLE WHILE I WAS ON VACATION, MOM?

GOODNESS, NO! WE BUILT A LITTLE THRONE FOR HER SO SHE COULD WATCH TV MORE COMFORTABLY!

Panel 2:
I BROUGHT HER BOWLS OF FRESHLY COOKED CHICKEN AND RICE THREE TIMES A DAY... YOUR FATHER TOOK HER TO THE PARK FOUR TIMES A DAY...

Panel 3:
...AND WE TOOK TURNS BRUSHING HER BEFORE WHEELING IN HER TOY SELECTION EACH MORNING.

Panel 4:
ELECTRA! AREN'T YOU HAPPY TO SEE ME??

YEAH, RIGHT...

ELECTRA · ELECTRA · ELECTRA

Panel 5:
YOU'RE BACK, CATHY! OH, THANK HEAVENS! YOU'RE BACK!

WHY? DID SOMETHING HAPPEN WHILE I WAS GONE?

CHARLENE

Panel 6:
ARE YOU KIDDING?! I HAD TO GO THROUGH THE WHOLE JULIA ROBERTS FIASCO WITHOUT YOU!! THEN DONALD DUMPED MARLA...THEN DONALD PROPOSED TO MARLA...

CHARLENE

Panel 7:
PRINCE CHARLES DIDN'T SHOW FOR DI'S 30TH BIRTHDAY...ROSEANNE BARR REMARRIED HER HUSBAND... PRINCESS CAROLINE WAS SPOTTED WITH VINCENT LONDON... MERYL STREEP HAD ANOTHER BABY GIRL AND ONE OF THE KENNEDYS HAD A TATTOO REMOVED!!

Panel 8:
DID ANYTHING HAPPEN THAT HAD ANYTHING TO DO WITH THE OFFICE?

NOT THAT I'M AWARE OF.

Panel 9:
I HANDLED THE WEISS CRISIS JUST THE WAY YOU WOULD HAVE, CATHY!

WHEW, THANKS! I WOULD HAVE HATED TO FACE THAT ONE AGAIN AFTER MY VACATION!

Panel 10:
FIRST I PUT IT IN MY "TO CALL" PILE... THEN I MOVED IT TO MY "TO WRITE TO" PILE... THEN I PUT IT BACK IN MY "TO CALL" PILE...

Panel 11:
THEN I BURIED IT IN MY "TO READ" PILE, WHERE IT WAS ACCIDENTALLY PICKED OUT AND ROUTED TO BRIAN, WHO LOST IT FOR TWO DAYS AND JUST RETURNED IT THIS MORNING!

Panel 12:
THE MENTOR PROGRAM BACKFIRES ONCE AGAIN.

I WENT ON VACATION. IT TOOK $900 AND TEN DAYS TO FORGET MY WORRIES.

I CAME HOME. IT TOOK NO MONEY AND 45 SECONDS TO FORGET MY VACATION.

SEE? YOU'RE ALREADY MORE EFFICIENT!

OH, PLEASE, ELECTRA... DON'T BE MAD AT ME! HERE... LET'S PLAY WITH YOUR TOYS! LET'S BRUSH YOUR HAIR! LET'S HAVE SOME SNACKS!

...UNBELIEVABLE. LOOK HOW MUCH HARDER I TRY WHEN YOU'RE ALOOF! WE ALL TRY HARDER TO PLEASE WHEN THE OTHER ONE'S ALOOF!

EH, I DON'T REALLY FEEL LIKE DINNER TONIGHT, IRVING.

GREAT! I'LL GO TO THE DRIVING RANGE!

CAN I HELP IT IF DOGS ARE BETTER AT HUMAN NATURE THAN HUMANS ARE?

I GAINED FIVE POUNDS ON MY VACATION! I CAN'T LET IRVING SEE ME THIS WAY!

CATHY, HE WAS WITH YOU ON VACATION! HE'S ALREADY SEEN YOU THAT WAY!

BUT HE HASN'T SEEN ME SINCE I FOUND OUT I GAINED IT!

HE WAS WITH YOU! HE WATCHED YOU GAIN IT!

BUT I LOOKED THINNER WHEN I DIDN'T KNOW I'D GAINED IT! I LOOK COMPLETELY DIFFERENT NOW!

READY FOR LUNCH, CATHY?

AACK!!

WHAT HAPPENED TO HER??

SEE? WHAT DID I TELL YOU?

120

TA DA! HERE HE IS! HIS NAME IS GUS!

GUS??

WE JUST GOT THE AMNIO RESULTS, SO WE KNOW HE'S A HEALTHY BABY BOY, DON'T WE, GUS?

OH, CATHY...ZENITH IS IN PRE-SCHOOL FOR GIFTED 2-YEAR-OLDS... LUKE RESTRUCTURED HIS BUSINESS SO HE CAN STUDY FRENCH WITH HER IN THE AFTER-NOONS...I'M DOING SALES FROM MY COMPUTER AT HOME, AND NOW WE'RE EXPECTING AN IN-CREDIBLE LITTLE BABY BOY!!

WHAT'S NEW WITH YOU?

YOU NAMED YOUR DAUGH-TER ZENITH, AND YOU'RE NAMING YOUR SON "GUS"??

DIFFERENT DECADE, CATHY. WHEN WE HAD ZENITH WE WERE IN THAT WHOLE '80s OVER-ACHIEVER YUPPIE THING...

...BUT GUS WILL BE OUR BABY FOR THE '90s! WHOLESOME... DOWN TO EARTH. A RETURN TO SIMPLE, HONEST FAMILY VALUES!

OF COURSE WE'RE RE-DOING OUR HOME IN KNOTTY COUNTRY PINE WITH HEIRLOOM QUILTS AND RUSTIC HAND-THROWN POTS FILLED WITH AZALEAS SNIPPED FROM MOMMY'S ORGANIC GAR-DEN WITH HER STAINLESS STEEL SMITH AND HAWKEN GARDENING SHEARS, GROWN IN THE RICH SOIL FROM DADDY'S SHARPER IMAGE COMPOST MAKER!

WHEW. WHAT A DEPAR-TURE.

I JUST CAN'T BELIEVE WE EVER USED TO BE SO MATERIALISTIC!

SALAD BAR

I ASKED FOR AN EX-TRA NAPKIN 10 MINUTES AGO!

IT'S RIGHT THERE.

DON'T TAKE IT PERSON-ALLY.

SHE'S STARTING HER FIFTH MONTH OF PREGNANCY, AND HER BER-SERK HORMONES ARE CAUSING HER TO BE MOODY, FORGETFUL AND CONGESTED.

SHE'S TOO BIG FOR REGULAR CLOTHES, BUT TOO SMALL FOR MATERNITY CLOTHES, MAKING HER FEEL SUSPENDED IN A SUR-REAL BLOATED SPACE WITH NOTH-ING TO REALLY "SHOW" FOR IT.

HOW MANY CHILDREN HAVE YOU HAD?

NONE OF MY OWN, BUT 23 OF MY GIRLFRIENDS'.

I KNOW YOU HAVE TO GET BACK TO THE OFFICE, CATHY, BUT WOMEN DON'T GET ENOUGH CHANCES TO STOP AND SEE THAT IT'S ALL REALLY POSSIBLE.

A BRILLIANT 30-MONTH-OLD DAUGHTER... A SON ON THE WAY... A NURTURING HUSBAND... ...A BUSINESS I CAN RUN FROM MY HOME....

I'VE DONE IT, CATHY! I HAVE IT ALL!!

...AND IT'S ALL SCREAMING, BROKEN OR FILTHY.

LUKE! WHAT ARE YOU DOING HERE? ZENITH WAS SUPPOSED TO BE AT HER PRESCHOOL YOUNG PEOPLE'S CONCERT UNTIL 2:00!

BY 11:15, ZENITH HAD TAKEN OFF ALL HER CLOTHES, BITTEN THE CONDUCTOR IN THE KNEE AND GOADED THE KLEIN TWINS INTO A SHRIEKING CONTEST.

COMING THIS SOON AFTER THE POTTERY WORKSHOP INCIDENT, HER TEACHER SAID SHE HAD NO CHOICE BUT TO, QUOTE, "EXPEL THIS LITTLE L-U-N-A-T-I-C!"

LUNATIC!

SHE'S TOO ADVANCED FOR THAT CROWD, ANYWAY.

SHE ISN'T POTTY-TRAINED YET, DEAR.

ZENITH BAD!

OH, NO, HONEY! YOU CAUSED A LITTLE RIOT AT PRESCHOOL BUT YOU AREN'T BAD!

MAYBE MOMMY HASN'T SPENT ENOUGH TIME WITH YOU... MAYBE MOMMY'S SPENT TOO MUCH TIME WITH YOU... MAYBE MOMMY'S SPENT THE RIGHT AMOUNT OF TIME BUT DID EVERYTHING WRONG!

MOMMY BAD.

MOMMY BAD?!!

NICE TO SEE YOU'RE GETTING THE MOTHER-DAUGHTER THING OFF TO A HEALTHY START, ANDREA.

Panel 1: NOW DADDY WILL PLAY WITH ZENITH WHILE MOMMY WORKS IN HER HOME OFFICE!

Panel 2: DADDY'S BEEN OUT OF HIS OFFICE FOR TWO HOURS! MOMMY WAS SUPPOSED TO DO HER WORK IN THE MORNING!

MOMMY SPENT THE MORNING SCRAPING PLAY-DOH OUT OF HER COMPUTER KEYBOARD!

Panel 3: IT ISN'T DADDY'S FAULT THAT MOMMY IS DISORGANIZED!

DADDY HASN'T TRIED TO CONDUCT BUSINESS WITH A TWO-AND-A-HALF-YEAR-OLD HANGING FROM HIS NECK!!

Panel 4: ANOTHER COUPLE CROSSES THE FINE LINE BETWEEN CARE-GIVING AND GUILT-GIVING.

Panel 5: WE HAVE A GIFTED 30-MONTH-OLD DAUGHTER WHO'S IN NEED OF A NEW DAY-CARE ARRANGEMENT, AND WE'D LIKE TO TOUR YOUR FACILITY.

YOU MUST BE JOKING.

Panel 6: WE'D PREFER A MORE EDUCATIONAL ENVIRONMENT, BUT MIGHT CONSIDER ONE WHERE SHE COULD SIMPLY HONE HER SOCIAL SKILLS.

OUR NEXT OPENING IS IN 1998.

Panel 7: PLEASE! TAKE HER! JUST TWO CRUMMY HOURS A DAY! ANYTHING! TAKE HER!

Panel 8: HOW'D YOU DO?

ZENITH IS OUT OF THE QUESTION, BUT OUR UNBORN SON CAN GO TO DAY CARE WHEN HE'S SEVEN.

Panel 9: IF I DON'T WORK, WE CAN'T PAY ALL OUR BILLS... IF I DO WORK, IT TAKES MOST OF WHAT I MAKE TO PAY FOR DAY CARE.

Panel 10: IF I DON'T WORK, I GET CLAUSTROPHOBIC AND CRANKY. IF I DO WORK, I FEEL LIKE I'M DESERTING HER.

Panel 11:

Panel 12: MOMMY'S ON THE GUILT-TRACK.

123

WE PLAYED MOZART TO ZENITH BEFORE SHE WAS BORN TO GIVE HER A FOUNDATION IN MUSIC... ...WE HUNG POSTCARDS FROM THE LOUVRE OVER HER CRIB TO ACQUAINT HER WITH THE ARTS...

WE'VE STUDIED EVERY BOOK ON THE EMOTIONAL AND INTELLECTUAL DEVELOPMENT OF A CHILD...

WE ARE **NOT** GOING TO HAND THIS LITTLE TREASURE OVER TO JUST **ANYONE** TO TAKE CARE OF!

ENGLISH! I MIGHT HAVE FOUND ONE WHO SORT OF SPEAKS ENGLISH!

HOW MUCH?

WELL, THAT'S THAT. IF A NANNY IS AVAILABLE, THERE'S ALWAYS SOME HIDEOUS REASON WHY.

SLAM!

IN THIS DAY AND AGE, IF SOMEONE'S STILL ON THE MARKET, THERE'S SOME HIDEOUS REASON WHY.

ANYTIME SOMEONE'S STILL OUT THERE LOOKING, THERE'S SOME HIDEOUS REASON WHY, AND THE EXACT SAME LAME EXCUSE!

MAYBE I JUST HAVEN'T FOUND THE RIGHT SITU- ATION YET!!

BINGO! HONESTLY, I'D ALMOST THINK YOU'D BEEN THROUGH THIS ONE YOUR- SELF, CATHY!

A FRIEND OF A FRIEND HEARD A RUMOR ABOUT THIS NEW HOME-CARE CENTER CALLED "GRANNY NANNIES". HELP ME ASK THE RIGHT QUESTIONS, CATHY!

ARE THEY LICENSED? ARE THEY EDUCATED? HOW DO THEY DISCIPLINE? HOW MANY CHILDREN PER ADULT? WHAT ARE THEIR REFERENCES? IS IT SAFE? IS IT CLEAN? IS IT A WHOLESOME, HEALTHY, HAPPY, CREATIVE ENVIRONMENT?

AACK! THAT'S MY MOTHER!

WOULD MY DAUGHTER TURN OUT ANYTHING LIKE HER??

I DIDN'T KNOW YOU WERE STARTING "GRANNY NANNIES," MOM!

NEITHER DID I, CATHY.

Granny Nannies

I WHISPERED THE IDEA AS A LITTLE JOKE TO FLO IN THE LADIES ROOM AT THE MALL.

Granny Nannies

Granny Nannies

...BY 6:00 THAT EVENING WE HAD 2400 APPLICATIONS, 150 BRIBE OFFERS AND 49 PARENTS STANDING ON THE PORCH CLUTCHING VIDEOS OF THEIR ADORABLE CHILDREN.

Granny

IF NECESSITY IS THE MOTHER OF INVENTION, DESPERATION IS THE GRANDMA.

YOU SET UP THIS WHOLE DAY-CARE CENTER IN A WEEK??

OH, NO, CATHY. UNLIKE YOUR MOTHER, I HAVE SEVEN ADORABLE GRANDCHILDREN OF MY OWN!

Granny Nannies

I ALWAYS KEEP THIS ROOM FILLED WITH TOYS FOR WHEN THEY COME TO VISIT.

Granny Nan

Granny Nannies

...SEE? THERE'S THEIR LITTLE MUSIC CORNER...THEIR READING CORNER...AND HERE'S A WALL DEVOTED TO THEIR DARLING LITTLE ART PROJECTS!

Granny Nannies

Toys Room

SORRY, MOM.

PEER PRESSURE NEVER GOES AWAY. IT JUST TAKES UP MORE SQUARE FOOTAGE.

Granny Nannie

Granny Nannies

PLEASE! PLEASE! PLEASE!

WHINING WILL GET YOU NOWHERE, YOUNG LADY!

Granny Nannies

PLEASE!

WE'RE NOT DISCUSSING IT UNTIL YOU CHANGE THAT TONE OF VOICE!

Granny Nannies

PLEASE!! BUMP ONE OF THOSE OTHER KIDS AND PUT MY DAUGHTER ON YOUR DAY-CARE LIST!!

Granny Nannies

SIGN UP

FLO'S VERY GOOD WITH CHILDREN.

THESE BIG ONES ARE TOUGH, THOUGH.

THPT!

Granny Nannies

SIGN UP

126

THE MORTGAGE BILL: DULL NAUSEA. DON'T WANT TO LOOK. DON'T WANT TO THINK ABOUT IT.

THE GAS BILL: TOTAL FUTILITY. THE PHONE BILL: NUMBING. INCOMPREHENSIBLE. NO FEELING WHATSOEVER.

...AACK! WHAT IS THIS??! THIS IS AN **OUTRAGE**!! THIS IS AN **OFFENSE**!! I AM NOT GOING TO STAND FOR THIS!!!

FEW THINGS CAN MAKE US COME ALIVE LIKE A CHRISTMAS CATALOG IN AUGUST.

128